FROM COW To ice Cream

A Photo Essay
by Bertram T. Knight

Children's Press

A Division of Grolier Publishing
New York London Hong Kong Sydney
Danbury, Connecticut

Created and Developed by The Learning Source

Designed by Josh Simons

Acknowledgments: We would like to thank all the people who helped with this book. Special thanks go to Blue Bell Advertising Agency, for all their efforts on our behalf, and to Irene and Mike at Luna Park, for their warm hospitality and technical assistance. Without their cooperation this book would not have been possible.

Photo Credits: Baskin Robbins: 4-5; Brown Communications, Inc.: 2 (left corner), 6 (right), 10-11, 13 (right), 32 (top center); Blue Bell Advertising Agency: 12, 14, 18, 20, 22, 24-25; California Strawberry Commission: 13 (left); Charles Harrington/Cornell University: 9; David Lynch-Benjamin/Cornell University: cover (left), 8; Dreyer's & Edy's Grand Ice Cream: 16-17, 26-27; Ken Karp: 21, 28-29, 32 (top left, top right, & bottom row); Rick Rickman/Häagen Dazs: 23 (bottom); Robert Egan: cover (right), 1, 3, 6 (left), 7, 15, 30-31, back cover; University of Wisconsin-Madison: 19; Warren Faubel/Häagen Dazs: 23 (top).

Note: The actual ice cream-making process often varies from manufacturer to manufacturer. The facts and details included in this book are representative of one way of producing ice cream today.

Library of Congress Cataloging-in-Publication Data
Knight, Bertram T.
   From cow to ice cream : a photo essay / by Bertram T. Knight.
       p.   cm. — (Changes)
   Summary: Describes in photographs and brief text the steps involved
in making the ice cream we buy at the market, ice cream parlor, etc.
   ISBN 0-516-20706-7   (IBSN 0-516-26066-9 pbk.)
   1. Ice cream, Ices, etc.—Juvenile literature. 2. Ice cream industry—Juvenile literature.
[1. Ice cream. Ices. etc. 2. Ice cream industry.]   I. Title.
TX795.K56   1997
637'.4—dc21   96-39327
                                       CIP
                                       AC

Printed in the United States of America
      10 R 06 05

Imagine a world without ice cream!

What would happen to the chips in chocolate chip mint or the swirls in raspberry swirl or the cherries in cherry vanilla?

And where would you sprinkle the sprinkles or drizzle all that thick, hot fudge?

But don't worry. As long as there are people and hot summer days, there will be ice cream.

But where does ice cream come from?

It begins with dairy cows and the milk they give.

Twice each day, the cows come in from the pasture to be milked by machine. Some of their fresh milk is sent off to an ice cream factory.

At the same time, far away, mountains of raw sugar wait in a warehouse. When an ice cream company places an order, the raw sugar goes . . .

. . . to a refinery. Here, it is cleaned and then gently melted down into a liquid. Sugar tankers haul it away.

Soon, both the milk and the liquid sugar reach the ice cream factory. They wait outdoors in large storage tanks until . . .

. . . all the delicious flavorings arrive. Now everything is ready. It is time to make ice cream.

First, the milk and sugar go into a vat, or tub. Here, a big steel blade blends them together into a basic ice cream mix.

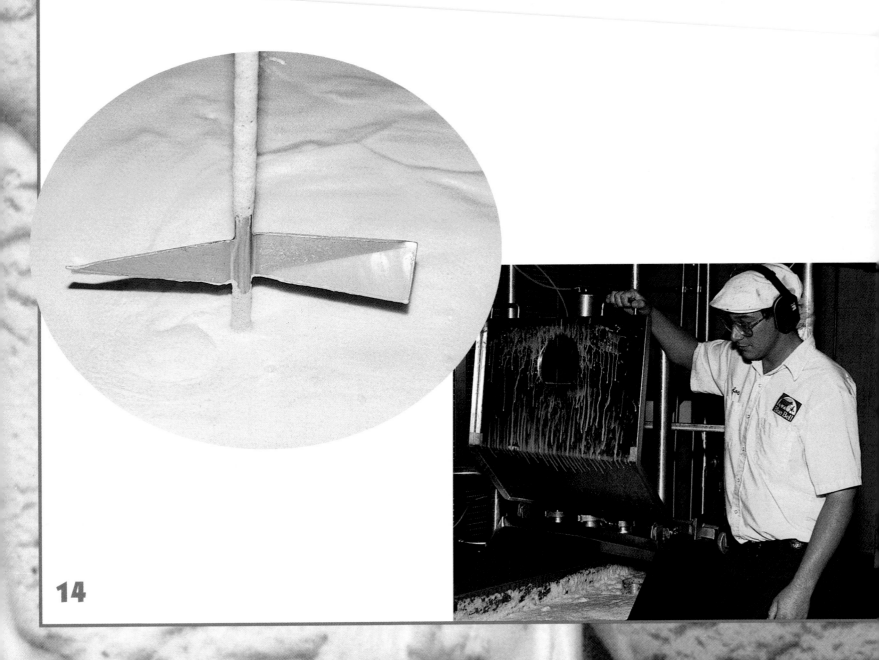

Now the mix is divided in two. Cocoa powder goes into one half. This makes a dark base for all the chocolatey flavors. The other half is the base for flavors like vanilla, peach, and chocolate chip mint.

A pasteurizer quickly heats and then cools each mix. This kills all harmful bacteria, or germs.

A homogenizer makes the mix smooth and even. Then it is cooled, stored, and given time to settle.

Now it's time for some taste and color. So, in go vanilla, chocolate sauce, and liquid fruit flavorings. The mix is beginning to look like ice cream.

A round freezer chills the mix and adds air bubbles. Without these bubbles, eating ice cream would be like chewing on ice cubes. The mix is now smooth, silky ice cream.

Here come the chunky flavorings! Fresh fruit adds chewiness to strawberry and cherry vanilla. Nuts give crunch to butter pecan and pistachio.

20

Best of all, chocolate chips, crumbled cookies, and even cookie dough get poured into the smooth ice cream.

Then quickly, before it melts, the ice cream is packed into containers . . .

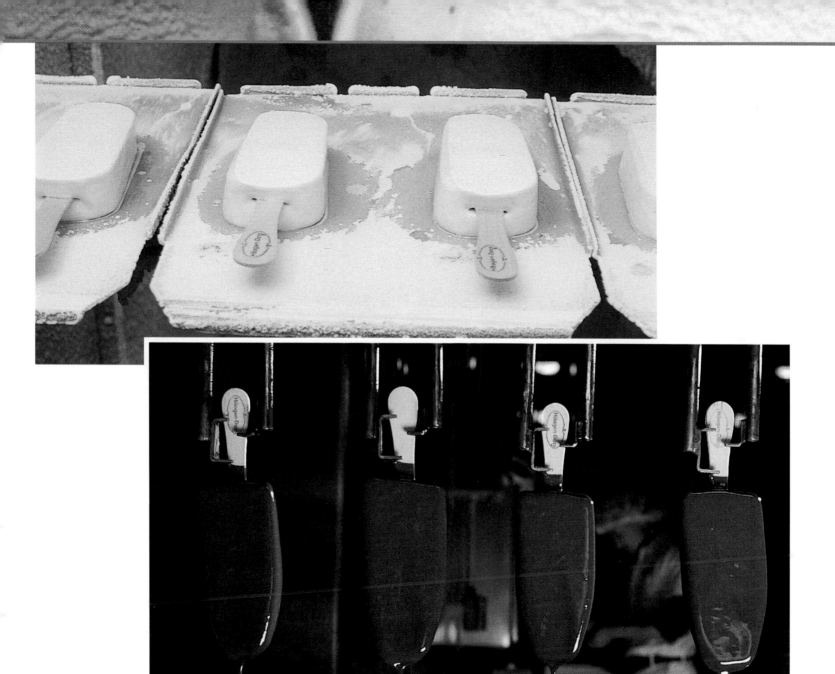

. . . or molded onto sticks and dipped in chocolate . . .

. . . or pressed between cookies for ice cream sandwiches.

To
Blast
Freezer
↓

Then everything is packed up and sent to an icy blast freezer. Here the ice cream will harden for hours.

But there's one more thing. Before leaving the factory, a sample from each batch must be tested. Does the ice cream taste the way it should? Is it the right color?

Finally, the ice cream goes into this giant refrigerator for cold storage. It stays there . . .

. . . until it is shipped to markets or ice cream stores like this one, near your home.

So, come in and choose your favorite flavor.

Then sit down and enjoy it . . .

. . . with your very best friends!

THE SCOOP ON ICE CREAM

Ice cream cones were invented at the 1904 World's Fair when an ice cream stand ran out of dishes. A waffle maker rolled a hot waffle into a cone shape, and the rest is history.

In the 1890s, ice cream sundays were sold only on Sunday. The spelling changed to **sundae** when people wanted to eat them every day of the week.

The first chocolate-covered **ice cream bar**, called the I-SCREAM BAR, was invented in 1921. It had no stick. By 1922 one million ice cream bars were sold every day!

Harry Burt put the first ice cream bar on a stick. He named it the **Good Humor** Ice Cream Sucker. Good Humor ice cream bars are still very popular.

The IT'S IT BAR, one of the first **ice cream sandwiches**, was sold in San Francisco during the 1920s. It was made with oatmeal cookies and vanilla ice cream.

Paper **Dixie Cups** were once called Healthy Kups. That's because they were thought to be cleaner and safer than metal cups.